<u>Handbook of Ocean Life</u>

By Edward Jacobson

Table of Contents

Intro

The ocean is one of the most unique places on earth. It covers about 70% of our planet, and each habitat is different, from the warm, tropical, life-filled coral reefs, to the cold, barren Arctic and Antarctic. There are many things we can learn from it that we could not from the land.

The blue whale, over 200 tons in weight

Chapter 1

Coral Reefs

Coral reefs are definitely one of the most diverse places on earth. They include a large variety of animals and plants. Despite how small they are they support one fourth of the life in the ocean. In this chapter we will cover coral reefs and the many species of life that live in them.

Brain Coral at Dusk

Coral

Although there are many life forms on coral reefs they are called *coral* reefs for a reason. The living structure that creates the reef deserves most of the credit for its beauty. Coral is a complex life form that, although we can only see its colorful outside, is full of a labyrinth of limestone skeleton. Without coral the reef would not exist, which makes it vital for the survival of the animals in the reef, which cannot manage without their home.

Staghorn coral

Coral mostly feeds on algae that grow within it, however at night the polyps stretch out their tentacles to feed on plankton drifting in the current. Coral faces many dangers too, including butterfly fish, humphead parrotfish, the crown of thorns seastar, and other coral in the infinite competition for space and food on the reef. Coral are definitely the most important animal on the reef, and should be protected.

Crustaceans

Mantis shrimp

Crustaceans are most common in coral reefs. This is probably because of the many hiding places, since they are on so many creatures' menu. Crustaceans are, like some of the other animals on the reef, commonly cleaners. Crustaceans are close to the bottom of the oceanic food chain. As you probably know crustaceans are most well known for their sharp pincers, a fierce defence when fighting for mates, but almost useless against predators. Some crabs are actually vital for coral, for they live in the coral and will fight off coral predators, such as the crown of thorns. Crustaceans play an important part in the food chain of the coral reefs, and should be treated with respect. We sometimes overfish lobsters, shrimp and crabs but, if we want coral reefs to stay healthy, we definitely shouldn't.

Fish

The most well known of all sea creatures is the fish. Out in the open ocean is where most fish roam, but on the coral reef there are also many fish, who are much more colorful than their open-water relatives. On the coral reef most fish are large and splattered with color. An example of a reef fish is the jack, capable of bursts of impressive speed.

A parrot fish

Most reef fish are at the bottom of the food chain, but some are nearly top predators, and they feed mostly on other fish.

Echinoderms

The most… odd looking creatures on the reef are echinoderms they include urchins and sea stars. The most well known of the two is the sea star, which can regrow limbs, and has no brain. To digest foods the sea star extrudes it's guts onto it's still living prey, a way we humans find rather revolting. Urchins sometimes scavenge the sea bed for dead animals and sometimes even attack sea stars. Echinoderms are one of the few predators that don't eat fish as their prey. Some echinoderms even eat each other.

Crown of thorns sea star

Echinoderms are unique, for they don't look like any other creatures on earth, so if they disappear there will be much less amazement and curiosity among humans in the future.

Mollusks

You probably know clams and oysters as just part of your seafood diner, but they are much more important on the reef. Bivalves are mostly filter feeders, but a few have become dangers that go beyond being a predator, such as the zebra oyster, an invasive species. Most bivalves are covered by a hard exoskeleton which protects the soft, delicate, vulnerable body. A lot of bivalves are tiny, but one exception is the giant clam, which is nearly 2 meters long, but strangely feeds only on plankton.

A giant clam

The other species of marine mollusks are gastropods they include sea snails and sea slugs. Gastropods mainly eat each other, yes, it seems strange but it's true, they eat their cousins. Despite their names, gastropods are not closely related to snails or slugs. We determine if they are a slug or a snail by their shell, if they have a shell they are a snail, if not they are a slug. Some slugs steal anemone's tentacles for defense. Mollusks are fascinating creatures that add a lot of excitement to the reef.

Cephalopods

Cephalopods are intelligent creatures with tentacles. Most cephalopods are hunters (the rank before top predators) in the food chain, but some are nearly at the very bottom.

An octopus

Octopuses are some of the most intelligent creatures in the sea. Some octopuses are very small, such as the blue ringed octopus, which can fit in the palm of your hand, while others are huge, including the giant pacific octopus, which can grow up to 4 meters long. Octopuses, like squids can shoot ink from their siphon as a defense against enemies, which include sharks. How it confuses them is simple, the ink will either make the water too murky for the octopus's predator to see clearly, or the ink will look like another octopus and the predator will attack the ink. Cephalopods are some of the most intelligent creatures in the sea, and not only that, but they have been around longer than fish, and should be treated with respect.

Chapter 2

Open Ocean

Despite how vast the open ocean is it's teaming with life of all shapes and sizes, from the tiny plankton, that we can only see with a microscope, to the huge blue whale, that is 100 ft. long. We have only explored a tiny fraction of the open ocean, but we are sure the mysteries it conceals are breathtaking.

The open ocean (a bird's eye view)

Schooling Fish

The most abundant creatures in the open ocean besides plankton are schooling fish. All schooling fish feed on plankton, occasionally form into large bait balls, and can be silver in color. Schooling fish in a bait ball often trigger feeding frenzies. These fast-paced scenes include many important roles, the lone hunter, the large hunter, the group hunters, the dive-bomb hunter, and the hunted. Some feeding frenzies include a few of one role, others don't include some of the roles but they all always have exactly one hunted, and that is the schooling fish.

Anchovies

Schooling fish are truly amazing. If we don't protect them they will become very sparse and we will regret that greatly.

Billfish

Billfish are some of the fastest fish in the sea. Named for their large bills, billfish are near top predators. Billfish's main prey consists of small schooling fish, such as herring. The three main types of billfish are marlins, sailfish, and swordfish. Each has a similar strategy, rush into the baitball, slash at a target stunning and/or injuring them, and finally, eat. Sailfish are the fastest fish, and the second fastest creatures in the world. They also change colors when they are excited.

A sailfish hunting

Swordfish are not as fast as sailfish, but they have a *much* longer bill, that allows them to more easily injure their prey. Marlins are big and bulky and often jump out of the water to catch fish. Billfish are important to the oceanic food chain and it will take a large step toward its collapse if they disappear.

Sharks

Sharks, despite what some people say, are not a danger to humans at all. However, they are top predators on their home turf. Most sharks' main prey are dolphins, seals and sea lions, fish, and other sharks. Some sharks are small, others are enormous.

A blue shark

The most well known sharks is the great white. Named for its white belly, the great white grows more than 20 feet long, and is the largest living predatory fish. Also very well known is the bull shark, which can survive in freshwater for a long time. The blue shark uses camouflage to ambush its prey, and is also very fast and sleek. The mako shark is very fast and sneaky. Hammerheads have, of course, hammer-shaped heads and come in many different species (they are almost as well known as great whites). Some sharks are hosts and allow pilot fish to swim next to them. Sharks are important and need to be protected, for they are threatened by humans much more than humans are threatened by them.

Jellies

Jellyfish are not the most complex creatures, but certainly fun to study. Most jellyfish eat microscopic copepods and other tiny crustaceans, but a few eat fish and some even other jellyfish. All jellyfish have no brain or heart, and are about 95% water. Most shallow water jellies have stinging tentacles used for killing prey and defending themselves. Jellyfish hunt by using just nerve and instinct, for they cannot think (the same is true for escaping predators that want to hunt *them*).

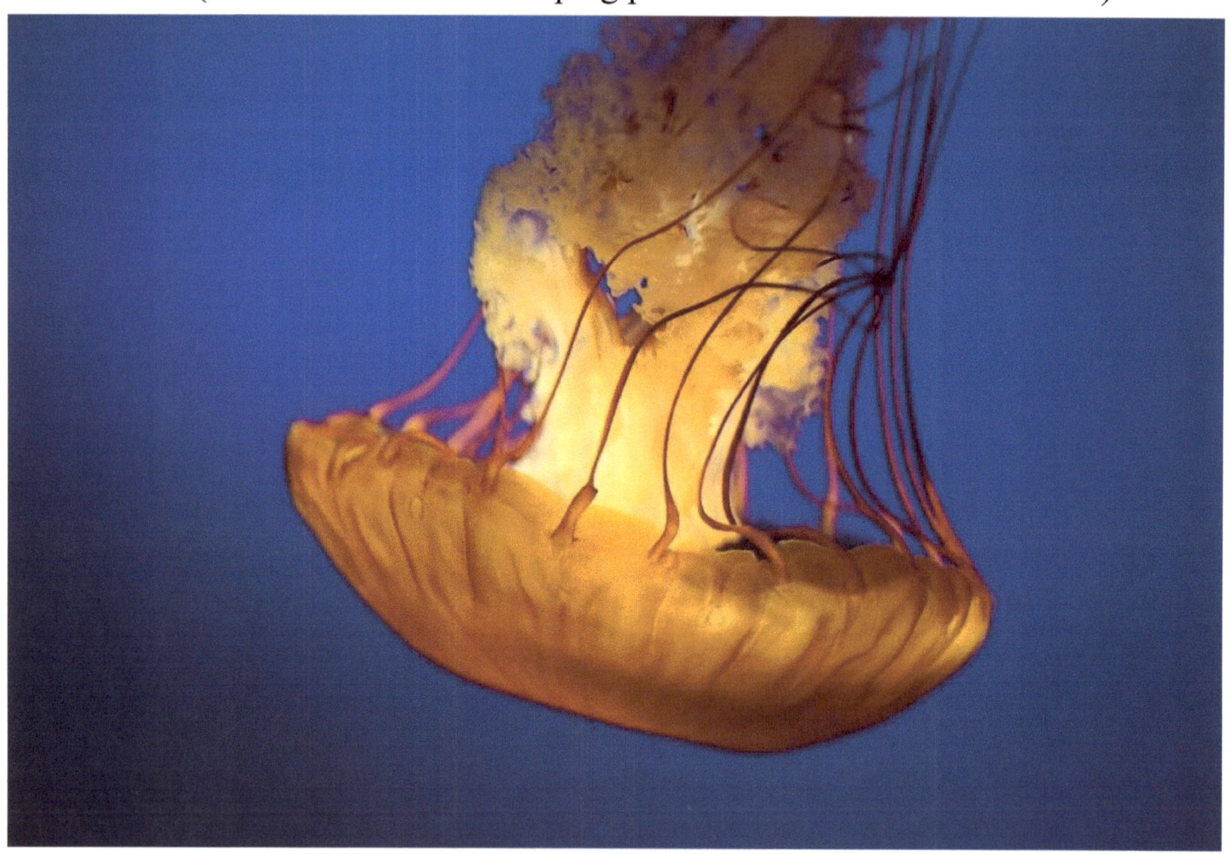

A jellyfish drifting down

Jellyfish are thought to be very dangerous however they are barely a threat to humanity at all. Sadly people still kill them out of hatred and fear, but if they continue some of the most fascinating creatures, that also have been on this earth since life started, will disappear.

Cetaceans

Whales and dolphins are highly intelligent creatures that are also efficient predators. They are (along with cephalopods) the most intelligent creatures in the world's oceans. Dolphins, unlike whales however, are very playful. Most dolphins use seaweed pieces as "toys" to play with when traveling. Dolphins have different ways of breathing, for example spinners jump out of the water and do graceful spins through the air, while others, such as the common dolphin, prefer to simply stick their blowhole out of the water. Most dolphins eat small fish and squid as their prey.

A pod of spinner dolphins

Baleen whales are much, much, *much* larger than dolphins and are also slower in most ways. They use low, loud rumbles as "songs" which are used to attract mates. All baleen whales eat small creatures (ex. plankton, krill, etc.) but can engulf hundreds of them in one mouthful. Whales and dolphins are incredible creatures.

Chapter 3

Deep Sea

The deep sea is *even* less explored than the open ocean, in fact, we couldn't reach it until the mid-20th century. All of its mysteries that we have discovered are breathtaking and we are sure we will think the same when we discover more.

A dumbo octopus

Fish (Deep Sea)

Deep sea fish are rare, and have much weirder habits than shallow-water fish. The most famous of deep sea fish is the anglerfish, which was one of the first ones to be studied. Named for the lure on the top of their head (which attracts prey with bioluminescent light), they are very well known. Female anglers are the only ones with a lure, and the males not only don't have the thing that identifies anglers for humans, but are only a fraction of the size of the female. They mate by the male biting at the female's underside until he is attached.

A fangtooth

Some other deep sea fish are less known, for example the fangtooth which has such large teeth that it can't close its mouth. Many other fish use bioluminescence to, some use them to escape, and some use them to ambush. People are already starting to fish creatures such as these, but if they continue they will later find they regret it.

Jellies (Deep Sea)

Deep sea jellies are much more "weird" than shallow-water ones. Some don't have stingers. Others produce light. The most well known deep sea jelly is the comb, which has streaks of color that run through its body, and, instead of stinging tentacles, they posses sticky ones, which grab copepods that drift along in the current.

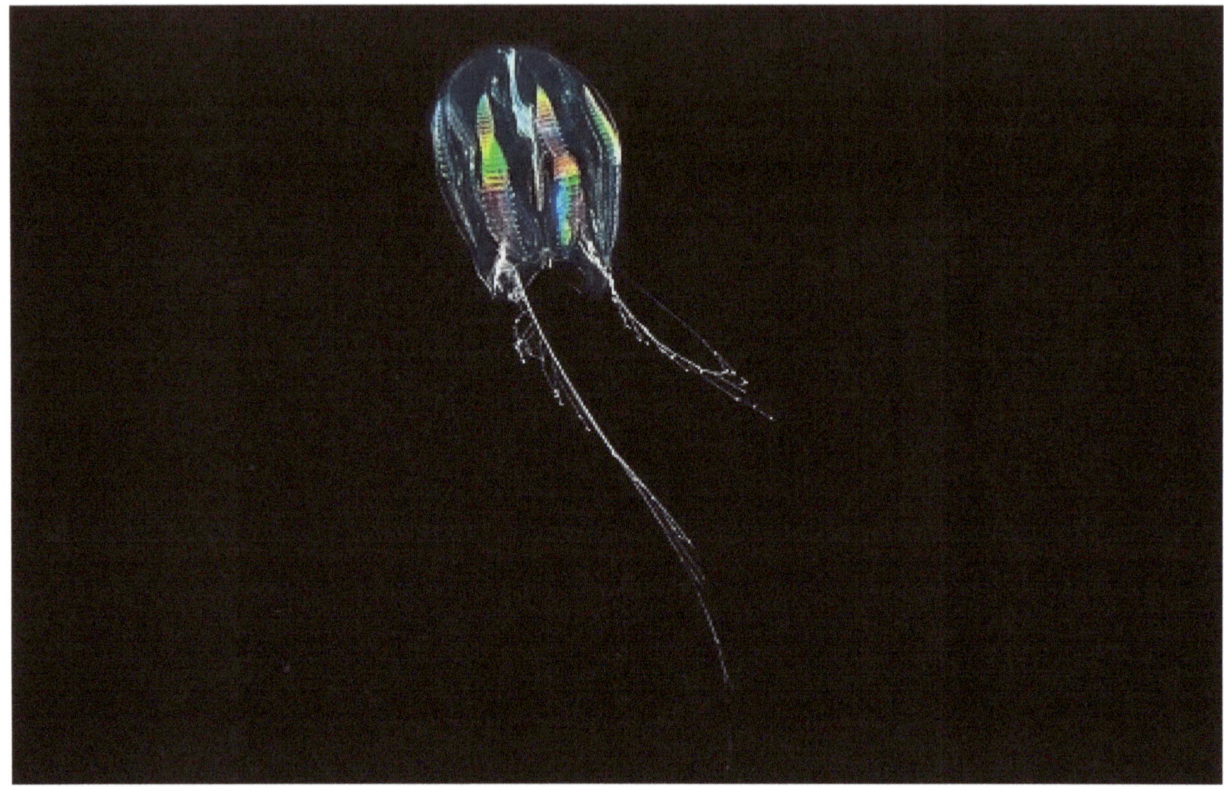

A comb jelly drifting along

Some deep sea jellies have adapted a red color, and no deep sea creature can see red, for they have spent their entire life in darkness so the jellies are safe from predators. Deep sea jellies are just as interesting as their shallow-water cousins and although they are not hunted now, they also need protection.

Cephalopods (Deep Sea)

Deep sea cephalopods are much less known than shallow-water ones, but are just as fascinating. One of the most famous ones is the vampire squid, named for the many "teeth" on its underside. Another famous one is the dumbo octopus, which was named after the disney character *Dumbo*, because of the large flaps that look like the character's ears.

A deep sea octopus

Also well known is the firefly squid. As its name states, its entire body glows (but especially the tentacles). Deep sea cephalopods are fascinating and any creature on earth with sense (and equal IQ to ours) would protect them.

Crustaceans (Deep Sea)

Deep sea crustaceans are fascinating creatures, and their habits are quite interesting and odd. Most deep sea crustaceans (like shallow-water ones) are the lowest in the food chain, for most of them feed entirely on "marine snow," drifting particles of dead plants and animals. Unlike shallow water crustaceans, most deep sea ones have learned how to swim, for they never touch an inanimate solid surface in their lives.

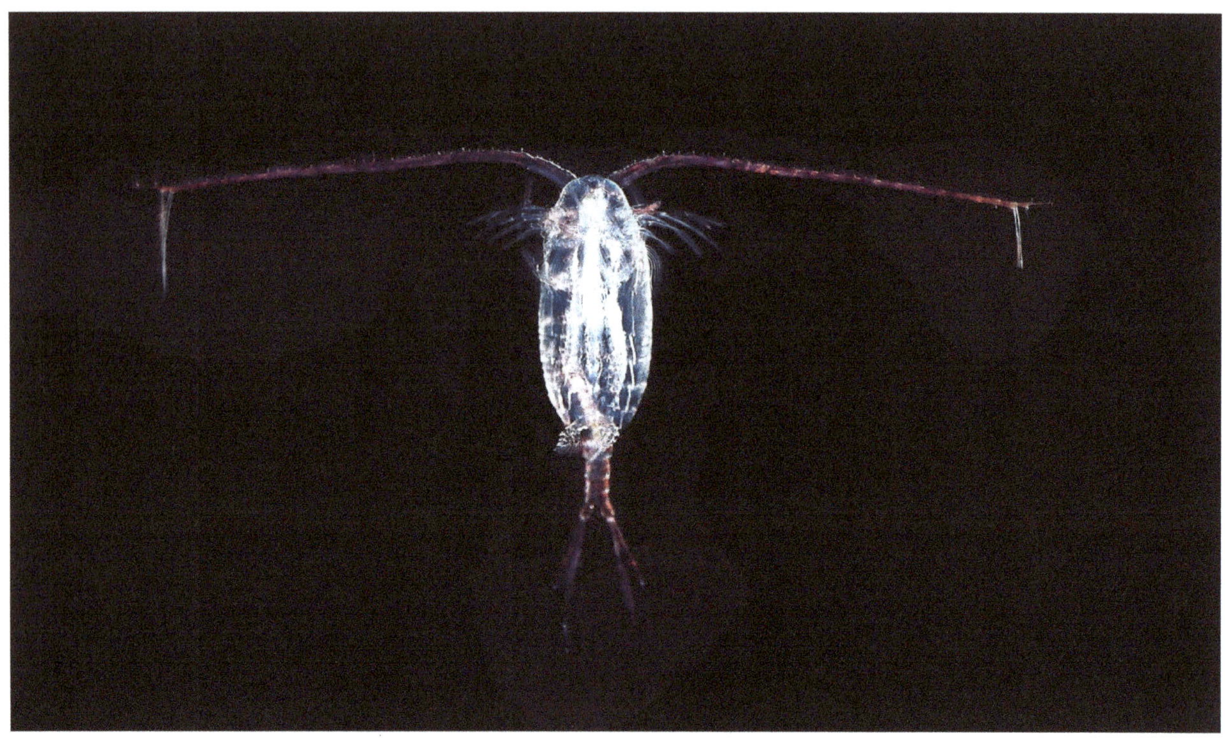

A deep sea copepod

Some deep sea crustaceans are regular size, for example the red prawn, others, such as the copepod, are tiny. Deep sea crustaceans are just as fascinating as shallow-water crustaceans, and should be protected.

Chapter 4

Coasts

Coasts are very interesting places. They have many animals living both on them, *and* in them. Some of their creatures are unique, and not found in the sea, others (cetaceans) would die beached, if they came out from the "big-blue".

The coast of the Galapagos

Shore Crabs

Shore crabs are interesting creatures. Some shore crabs are more closely related to their seagoing relatives, and have to return to shallow waters to breathe, while others, such as the ghost crab, have adapted to breathing on land. Most shore crabs dig in the sand to find small animals buried in it.

A ghost crab

Shore crabs are common prey of animals such as seabirds. A lot of them make burrows to hide in when predators are prowling about. They, like a few shallow water crustaceans, have very "tall" eyes. Shore crabs are just as fascinating as seagoing ones, and also just as important.

Seals and Sea-Lions

Seals and sea-lions are common mammals. As well as being excellent swimmers, they spend a lot of time on the shore. Their main predators are sharks and orcas, and they are often pursued by them. Seals also live in the Arctic and Antarctic (see chapter six). Most seal pups suckle for a short amount of time.

A Californian sea-lion on shore

Sea-lions have comparatively larger whiskers than seals. Like seals, their common prey is small fish and squid. They will spend large amounts of time on shore, slightly more time than seals.

Hidden Creatures

Although it would appear that most coasts are deserted (besides the occasional crab), actually they are teeming with life. Microscopic creatures and a few worms are hidden *within* the sand. They feed mostly on each other. Worms come out when the tide has dropped. The sand washes away giving them easy access to food. Many animals, including crabs, snails, and worms, feed on these creatures. They play as the plankton of the shore, teeming but invisible to the naked eye.

Some shore sand, which likely has many creatures hidden in it.

These creatures act as the base of the carnivorous food chain on shores and are as important to that habitat as plankton are to the ocean.

Chapter 5
Arctic and Antarctic

The Polar regions of the world are some of the most diverse, from the small creatures living in the faint glow of the underside of the ice, to the giant whales slowly and elegantly breaching. Although we find this one of the hardest places to reach due to the freezing conditions, we can still explore it, and chances are it will have many astonishing things to discover.

A view of the antarctic.

<u>Penguins</u>

Penguins are mainly found in the antarctic, and not at all in the arctic. Probably the most well-known penguin is the Emperor Penguin. This penguin gives us an image used universally for all penguins. In fact there are penguins that have a drastically different look. The Adélei, for example, are much shorter and have an almost entirely black head (including the beak). Two white circles on each side of their head hold their eyes. There are many other similar penguin species with their own looks

To feed, penguins jump at high speeds into the water, and swim like torpedos, grabbing small fish and krill with their beaks. Since chicks have a fuzzy down that prevents them from swimming, they cannot accompany their parents, so the parents hire "babysitters," penguins that will protect the chicks until they return.

An Emperor on the ice.

As soon as the adults return, they regurgitate their food into the chicks' mouths. Penguins' main natural predators are Leopard Seals and Orcas. Penguins are truly fascinating creatures, no matter what the type from Adélies to Emperors.

Seals and Sea-Lions (Polar)

As well as being found on coasts, (see chapter 4) seals and sea-lions are also found in the polar regions. One of the only seals in the Antarctic is the Leopard Seal, which, as mentioned on the previous page, eats penguins. They act as sharks for the Antarctic, since there are no actual sharks there. Meanwhile, in the Arctic, seals and sea-lions are more abundant, and act as essential part of the Arctic food chain. They come in many varieties. Some examples include Harp Seals, Ringed Seals, Ribbon Seals, and Spotted Seals. One of the oddest seals in the arctic is the Hooded Seal. The males have a big black nose, and have an inflatable red "ball" on their that they can blow up and bob around.

A young harp seal.

Arctic seals' main predators are polar bears, but lucky for these seals, polar bears can barely dive, whereas they are excellent swimmers and dart quickly out of the reach of the bears.

Cetaceans (Polar)

Many cetaceans migrate to the Antarctic and Arctic in the summer, when the ice has cleared away, for the great abundance of food and nutrients found in the area. Others *live* in the poles. Some are deadly hunters, such as the Orca. Others, filter feeders, such as the Bowhead whale, named for it's huge head, which is nearly the size of a two-car garage. Both find a rich supply of food in this environment. Most of these cetaceans are whales, the only dolphin that makes its habitat in these harsh conditions is the Orca, but there are many dolphin size whales, such as the beluga and the narwhal.

A Bowhead whale.

These elegant giants show us the importance of exploring the poles.

Fish (Polar)

Fish not only flourish in the open ocean and coral reefs, but also at the top and bottom of the world. Many fish in the poles feed on the abundance of microscopic creatures found only in these landscapes. Some fish, including the ice fish survive the extreme temperatures of the poles by the adaptation of having antifreeze in their blood.

An ice fish.

These fish's main predators are mostly large mammals, like seals, orcas, and whales. They are essential to the ecosystem.

Chapter 6

Other Undersea Places

Alongside the main habitats there are also many minor, lesser known habitats, including seagrass beds, kelp forests, and sea mounds. In this chapter, you will learn about the other habitats, and their importance, despite their lesser quantities and publicity.

A patch of seagrass

Seagrass Beds

Seagrass is short kelp that forms in beds. Like kelp, seagrass has several different variants. The most common is turtle grass. Seagrass beds have lots of life in them, including Turtles, Dugongs, Manatees, Seahorses, Sea Dragons, Flounders, Starfish, Urchins, and Queen Conches. All of this life either feeds on the seagrass, or feeds on the creatures that feed on the seagrass. Manatees and Dugongs used to get confused for mermaids, because of the shadow they created, but actually resemble grey cows. Ironic, isn't it?

A Dugong

Seagrass beds are known as the plains of the ocean, and though they are not breathtakingly beautiful, they are important nonetheless.

<u>*Kelp Forests*</u>

Kelp forests are, as you would guess, huge areas built around kelp that resemble a forest. Kelp forests flourish with life and are filled with many different creatures, from tiny crustaceans to large sharks. Kelp forests are good hiding places for small fish, and offer sanctuary from large predators. Sea urchins prey on the bases of the kelp in the forests, but they are often stopped by sea otters, who eat them.

A kelp forest

Sea urchins are a real threat to kelp forests, and if it wasn't for otters the kelp forests might not exist. Otters are an excellent example of how nature can care for itself.

Mangrove Forests

Mangroves are unique places where the roots of the mangrove trees are submerged under water instead of underground. These small areas are usually surrounded by mud, so there aren't many creatures on the shore. During low tide, there is limited oxygen in the waters of the mangrove forests, which gives advantages to aquatic mammals hunting in the area, however there is also a fish that has adapted to the Mangrove forests, the lungfish, a fish that has lungs and gills, so that it can take oxygen from the air as well as the water.

The roots of a mangrove tree.

Mangrove forests are amazing and unbelievable places.

Sea Mounds

Sea mounds are the underwater part of young islands. Since they are only found in the open ocean, and are packed with plants and animals alike, they are sort of like oases in an desert of nothing but water. They have a wide array of life. Turtles, sea stars, fish and sharks can all be found around sea mounds. The current brings waters rich with phytoplankton and zooplankton, which attract small fish, who in turn attract large fish, which then attract top predators. Also lots of algae grows there, perfect food for small shellfish.

A disguised crab on a sea mound

Sea mounds are beautiful places and are important the entire oceanic ecosystem.

Prehistoric Sea

Before land creatures even existed there were sea creatures. Fish, and undersea invertebrates ruled the world as the dominant life form. The most common fish was the lobe finned fish, but now only two exist, the lungfish and the coelacanth. It was from lobe finned fish that amphibians evolved. There were many crazy and kooky critters in the old days, like the Dunkleosteus, with its ridiculous "teeth", and the extremely common trilobite, which resembled a modern horseshoe crab.

What the Devonian sea might have looked like.

Though the prehistoric seas are no longer around there are many things we can learn from them through fossils and research.

Chapter 7

Oceans and Us

With the arrival of humans, oceans have been heavily influenced, in both good ways and bad. Not only do we need to know how we help and harm the oceans. By researching the oceans we learn why they wouldn't need us if we didn't make them need us.

A scuba diver

SCUBA and Submarines

SCUBA was Jacques Cousteau's invention. It stands for Self-Contained Underwater Breathing Apparatus, and was one of the most successful, easy-to-use, diving suits ever. SCUBA allows people to stay underwater for long periods of time, without a container or line. SCUBA has assisted hugely in the research of the ocean, much more efficient than the stereotype golden diving suit with a small "window" on the front, or submarines, when it comes to shallow-water diving.

A scuba diver

However, submarines are the only option when it comes to deep-water diving, as humans can't handle the pressure down there. One thing they have in common is both SCUBA and submarines have assisted in the research and protection of our oceans.

Pollution

Pollution kills many sea creatures daily it's the result of trash thrown in the ocean. If we don't do something soon about pollution, all coral reefs will die, most fish will die, and perhaps all air-breathing sea creatures. Some things that you can do to prevent this is to reuse your trash, perhaps turn that piece of cardboard into something more entertaining or useful.

Trash in the ocean

Pollution can be solved through rigorous work, and doing so could save our oceans.

Fishing

Fishing is okay, when done reasonably. Rod fishing is a good example, reasonable, controlled, beneficial, if for food, not for sport. However mass fishing is a serious problem, thousands of fish can be killed at once, and many other sea creatures will get caught in nets and suffocate. Schooling fish used to gather by the billions, but overfishing stopped that, and now the top number of a gathering will be a couple million, which is a lot, but no where near a billion.

Overfishing at work

We need to prevent this, and one way is to not fish in the wild, but in areas in which you may catch farmed fish, for it is not supporting mass fishing.

Conservation

Though humans are responsible for most if not all environmental issues when it comes to the ocean, some people are helping to make a change and protect the ocean. One way they do this is to create protected areas, where it is illegal to fish or dump trash. Another helpful strategy to protect sea life is captive breeding. They breed endangered species in captivity to let them flourish and protect them from predators.

Aquariums are good places for captive breeding.

Be like these people helping to protect the oceans and find your own way to save the lives of sea animals.

About the Author

Edward "Teddy" Robert Jacobson is an avid explorer of undersea worlds at 11, soon 12 years of age. For years he has researched deeply on this enlightening topic. When he's not studying the ocean, he enjoys reading Tolkien, watching Doctor Who and building with Lego bricks. He's written three books and a blog. He lives with his family in Loveland, Colorado.

Edward at home.